NORTH CAROLINA

Past and Present

Kristi Lew

rosen publishing's
rosen central

New York

For my North Carolina friends and family

Published in 2011 by The Rosen Publishing Group, Inc.
29 East 21st Street, New York, NY 10010

Copyright © 2011 by The Rosen Publishing Group, Inc.

First Edition

Library of Congress Cataloging-in-Publication Data

Lew, Kristi.
North Carolina: past and present / Kristi Lew. — 1st ed.
   p. cm. — (The United States: past and present)
Includes bibliographical references and index.
ISBN 978-1-4358-9491-4 (library binding) — ISBN 978-1-4358-9518-8 (pbk. book) — ISBN 978-1-4358-9552-2 (6-pack)
1. North Carolina—Juvenile literature. I. Title.
F254.3.L49 2011
975.6—dc22

2009054264

Manufactured in Malaysia

CPSIA Compliance Information: Batch #S10YA: For further information, contact Rosen Publishing, New York, New York, at 1-800-237-9932.

On the cover: Top left: One of the Civil War's largest naval battles was fought at Fort Fisher, near Wilmington, North Carolina. Top right: Today, downtown Raleigh, North Carolina's capital city, bustles with activity. Bottom: Pilot Mountain.

Contents

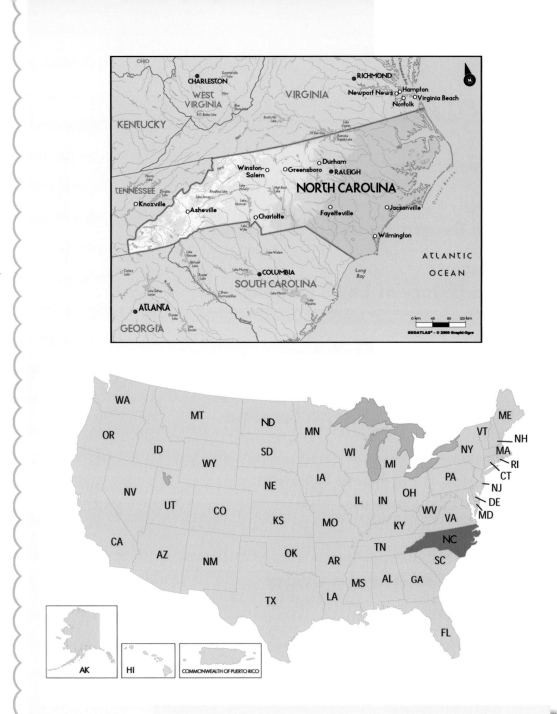

North Carolina lies on the East Coast of the United States. At 560 miles (901 kilometers) long, it is the longest state east of the Mississippi River.

Introduction

North Carolina is bordered to the east by the Atlantic Ocean. Small coastal towns line the state's 130-mile (209-kilometer) chain of barrier islands known as the Outer Banks. Behind the Outer Banks lie large, shallow bodies of water called sounds. North Carolina shares its western border with Tennessee. It's bordered to the north by Virginia and to the south by South Carolina. The state's southwestern tip adjoins Georgia.

Closer to the center of the state is an area called the Piedmont. This region is the home of North Carolina's largest city, Charlotte, which has more than half a million residents. The cities of Winston-Salem, Greensboro, and High Point, also referred to as the Triad, are located nearby. The state's capital and second largest city, Raleigh, lies to the east of these cities. Along with the cities of Durham and Chapel Hill, Raleigh makes up a part of the state known as the Triangle.

In 1629, King Charles I gave the territory of Carolina to his attorney general, Sir Robert Heath. In 1710, the colony was split into two sections. The southern section would eventually become the state of South Carolina. The northern portion became North Carolina, which came to be called the Old North State.

Inhabitants of North Carolina are sometimes called Tar Heels. This nickname most likely originated during the colonial period in reference to one of the state's major products: tar. According to some stories, the term "Tar Heel" came about when workers tracked spilled tar, leaving black footprints in their wake. Other stories claim the nickname was acquired during the Civil War (1861–1865), when a group of North Carolinians was left to fight alone by soldiers from another state. When the North Carolina soldiers met up with the deserters at a later date, they threatened to put tar on the heels of the retreating soldiers so that they would "stick" through the battle next time. North Carolina is sometimes called the Tar Heel State.

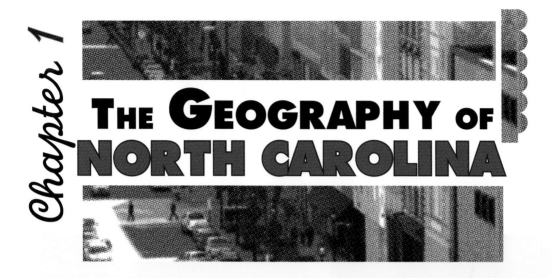

Chapter 1

THE GEOGRAPHY OF NORTH CAROLINA

Many people visit North Carolina every year, drawn by the state's natural beauty and mild climate. North Carolinians are proud of their state, which is home to a wide variety of terrain, from pristine beaches in the east to rugged mountains in the west. The 560-mile-long (901 km) state is the longest one east of the Mississippi River.

The Mountains

The mountains in North Carolina are part of the Appalachian Mountain range. The Appalachian Mountains stretch from Newfoundland in Canada to central Alabama, and they are the oldest mountains in the United States. The Blue Ridge Mountains and the Great Smoky Mountains are part of this mountain range. Parts of both of these sections run through the western area of North Carolina. North Carolina's western border runs through the Great Smoky Mountains National Park, the most visited national park in the country. The Great Smoky Mountains, also called the Smokies, are part of the Blue Ridge Mountains. The highest mountain in North Carolina, as well as the entire Appalachian chain, is Mount Mitchell in Yancey County. At 6,684 feet (2,037 meters), Mount Mitchell is not only the highest point in North Carolina, but it is also the highest peak east of the Mississippi River.

Many hikers climb to the top of Looking Glass Rock, near Brevard, North Carolina, to enjoy the beautiful views that the Appalachian Mountains have to offer.

The Outer Banks and the Coastal Plain

The lowest point in North Carolina is at the eastern end of the state, where the land meets the sea. The Outer Banks are a group of islands that lie just offshore. These barrier islands help protect the mainland from storms that originate in the Atlantic. Along the coast of North Carolina, three capes—Cape Hatteras, Cape Lookout, and Cape Fear—jut out into the ocean.

The waters off of North Carolina's Outer Banks are very shallow and treacherous. This area is also where the cold Labrador Current intersects with the warm waters of the Gulf Stream. The strong currents and severe weather created by this collision, as well as the navigational hazards of shallow water, have conspired to destroy thousands of ships. These shipwrecks have given this area a nickname: the Graveyard of the Atlantic. Today, lighthouses on North Carolina's coast provide assistance to mariners attempting to safely make their way through these waters.

The Cape Hatteras Lighthouse is the tallest lighthouse in the United States. It has been helping sailors navigate the shallow waters around the cape for more than one hundred years.

Inland of the Outer Banks lie the coastal plains. The coastal plains are low-lying, flat areas that include thick pine forests and numerous rivers, streams, and wetlands. North Carolina's wetlands are home to many native plants and animals. They also absorb water during storms, protecting neighboring areas from flooding. Many of the state's farms are located in the coastal plains.

Piedmont

Between the coastal plains and the mountains lies a region called the Piedmont. In French, the word "piedmont" means "foot of the

Roanoke Island

In 1587, English settlers founded a colony on the Outer Banks at Roanoke Island. Shortly after establishing the colony, a little girl named Virginia Dare became the first child of English parents born in the New World. In the summer of that year, John White, the leader of the expedition and Dare's grandfather, returned to England intending to bring much-needed supplies back to the colony. However, when White arrived in England, he found the country at war with Spain. Because all of England's ships were needed for the war effort, White was unable to return to Roanoke for three years. In 1590, when he again arrived on the island, he discovered all the colonists were gone. The only trace they left behind was the word "Croatoan" carved into the bark of a tree.

Today, the outdoor drama *The Lost Colony* tells the story of Virginia Dare's birth and the mysterious disappearance of the colonists. Written by Pulitzer Prize–winning playwright and North Carolina native Paul Green, the play was the first outdoor drama of its kind in the United States. First performed on July 4, 1937, near the site of the failed colony, it is also the longest-running outdoor historical drama in the country.

However, *The Lost Colony* is only one of the attractions that draw visitors to this 8-mile-long (13 km), 2-mile-wide (3 km) island. Vacationers often enjoy seeing the native animals, including sharks, sting rays, alligators, and sea turtles, that are housed in the island's branch of the North Carolina Aquarium. The island is also home to an offshoot of North Carolina's Maritime Museum, where visitors can learn about traditional fishing and boatbuilding methods used in the state. The museum also features a replica of the 1877 screw pile lighthouse that once guided mariners through Croatan Sound.

mountain." This area of the state is also called the foothills and is characterized by gently rolling hills ranging in elevation from 300 feet (91 m) in the east to 1,500 feet (457 m) in the west.

Six of the state's largest cities, including Charlotte, Raleigh, and Greensboro, are located in the Piedmont region. The area where the Piedmont meets the coastal plains is called the Sandhills. The Sandhills are famous for their championship golf courses and world-class horse breeders, train-ers, and stables.

Raleigh is North Carolina's capital and second largest city. It lies in the Piedmont region of the state.

North Carolina's Climate

North Carolina has a generally pleasant climate characterized by relatively mild winters and warm, humid summers. The coldest temperature ever recorded in North Carolina was -34 degrees Fahrenheit (-37 degrees Celsius) at the peak of Mount Mitchell on January 21, 1985. However, the rest of the state rarely gets that cold. The average winter low temperature is 27.3°F (−2.6°C). The hottest temperature ever recorded was 110°F (43°C) in Fayetteville on August 21, 1983.

Summer temperatures are greatly influenced by elevation. On top of Mount Mitchell, for example, the average afternoon temperature in mid-July is around 68°F (20°C). However, cities in the interior of the state, such as Fayetteville and Goldsboro, may routinely see high temperatures of more than 92°F (33°C) in the summer. Therefore, the average high temperature for the state is 88.3°F (31.3°C).

Animals of North Carolina

A variety of animals are found in North Carolina. The mountainous regions of the state provide a perfect habitat for animals such as beavers, black bears, boars, bobcats, and many others. In fact, the Great Smoky Mountains are the home of more species of salamander than anywhere else in North America.

The Outer Banks is one of the few places where wild horses still roam free. These horses are the descendants of Spanish mustangs that were brought over by European settlers. The coastal wetlands are home to alligators, bald eagles, and black bears. Many types of fish and other aquatic animals live in and around the state's coastal marshes, as well as in the open waters of the Atlantic Ocean, including the channel bass and the Southern Appalachian brook trout. Several threatened or endangered animals also live in North Carolina, including the bald eagle, eastern cougar, gray bat, piping plover, red wolf, roseate tern, and several species of sea turtles.

Plants of North Carolina

North Carolina is home to more than 120 types of trees, including the dogwood tree and the pine tree. One of the most unique plants found in the state is the Venus flytrap. Although now grown in many areas of the world, the Venus flytrap is native only to the

The carnivorous Venus flytrap is native to North Carolina's coastal plains. Its jawlike leaves capture and digest small animals, mainly spiders and insects.

coastal plains of North and South Carolina. This meat-eating plant snaps up insects in its traplike leaves. The trap seals shut to allow the plant to digest the insect, then it reopens in about three to fourteen days, ready to capture its next meal. Unfortunately, the Venus flytrap is in danger of disappearing from the wild. Other North Carolina plants that are threatened or endangered include the Blue Ridge goldenrod, the green pitcher plant, sea beach amaranth, and the smooth coneflower.

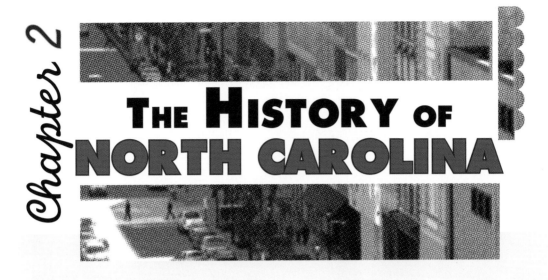

Chapter 2

THE HISTORY OF NORTH CAROLINA

When European settlers arrived in North Carolina in the 1580s, there were already a number of Native American tribes living there. These tribes included the Catawba, the Cherokee, the Tuscarora, and the Waccamaw. The Cherokee tribe was located in the western mountainous region of the state. The Catawba and Waccamaw settled in the Piedmont, and the Tuscarora made their home in the eastern coastal plains.

The Colonial Period

In 1653, sixty-six years after the disappearance of the Lost Colony, English settlers once again made their home in the state—this time permanently. Ten years later, King Charles II of England gave the land called Carolina, in honor of King Charles I, to eight Englishmen who had helped him regain the throne. These men were called the Lords Proprietors.

Although the area was split into two sections, north and south, in 1710, it would remain under the power of the Lords Proprietors or their descendants until 1729. At this time, seven of the eight Lords Proprietors sold their portion of Carolina back to King

George II. North Carolina was once again a royal colony and would remain as such until 1775, the beginning of the American Revolutionary War.

Revolutionary War

The first battle of the Revolutionary War to be fought in North Carolina occurred at Moore's Creek Bridge, near the city of Wilmington, on February 27, 1776. In this battle, loyalists to the British Crown faced about one thousand patriots who had partially dismantled

The towne of Pomeiock and true forme of their howses, couered and enclosed some with matts, and some with barcks of trees. All compassed abowt with smale poles stuck thick together in stedd of a wall.

When European settlers arrived in North Carolina, they encountered several Native American tribes living in the area. This 1585 sketch shows the Native American village of Pomeiooc.

the bridge during the night. Although they were outnumbered, the patriots, armed with cannons and muskets, managed to overpower the broadsword-carrying loyalists. Encouraged by this victory, the colonists voted in favor of independence from Britain, making the North Carolina colony the first to do so. Another victory on Sullivan's Island, near Charleston, South Carolina, convinced the other twelve colonies to do the same. All thirteen colonies officially declared their independence from Britain on July 4, 1776. North Carolina joined the Union on November 21, 1789, making it the twelfth state to do so.

In one of the largest naval battles of the Civil War, the Union Army captured Fort Fisher, on January 15, 1865. This served to cut off one of the Confederacy's last supply routes.

Civil War

Like many southern states during the eighteenth and nineteenth centuries, North Carolina relied on slave labor to build its economy. Slaves tended crops, performed household chores, and carried out many other jobs—all without pay. In 1830, hoping to prevent slaves from demanding freedom, North Carolina leaders passed a law prohibiting anyone from teaching a slave to read or write. Even stricter laws, preventing free blacks from going to school, voting, or preaching in public, were passed in 1835. In 1850, the southern states passed the Fugitive Slave Act. This act denied runaway slaves the right to a trial by jury and stated that slaves could not speak on their own behalf. It also declared that the U.S. marshals and all citizens were obligated to aid in the capture and return of runaway slaves.

In 1860, disagreements over slavery and other political issues caused eleven southern states, including North Carolina, to leave the United States. After seceding from the Union, they formed the Confederate States of America. North Carolina officially joined the Confederacy on May 20, 1861, making it the last southern state to do so. After years of fighting, the Civil War ended in 1865. The Confederacy surrendered to the Union, and slavery was abolished. North Carolina was readmitted to the Union in 1868.

Hard Times

In 1917, the United States entered World War I (1914–1918). More than eighty-five thousand young men from North Carolina served in the war. North Carolinians who were left at home did all they could to help the war effort. Women joined organizations like the Red Cross and the Salvation Army. Many went on to serve as nurses in military hospitals at home and abroad. Others bought war bonds to raise money for the war effort.

In 1929, the United States entered the Great Depression. Triggered by a stock market crash, this worldwide economic depression lasted nearly a decade. Unemployment soared as people lost their jobs. Money was scarce. To provide jobs for the unemployed, President Franklin D. Roosevelt established the Civilian Conservation Corps (CCC) in 1933. In North Carolina, men working with the CCC built the state's portion of the Appalachian Trail, a 2,178-mile (3,505-km) hiking trail that stretches from Georgia to Maine. The CCC also began building the Blue Ridge Parkway, one of the state's largest tourist attractions.

Old Salem

In 1733, a group of settlers called the Moravians fled Europe. They intended to establish a home in the New World, where they could practice their religion without persecution. By 1741, they had settled in the area of present-day Pennsylvania, creating a community that they called Bethlehem.

In Moravian communities, people lived in groups called choirs. People in the same choir ate, lived, studied, and attended church services together. At a young age, children left their parents and joined a Little Boys' Choir or a Little Girls' Choir. When the children turned twelve years old, they moved to the Older Boys' Choir or the Older Girls' Choir. When they turned nineteen, they joined either the Single Sisters' Choir or the Single Brethren Choir. When they got married, they became part of the Married People's Choir.

In 1753, twelve single men left Bethlehem and traveled to North Carolina, where they settled on a nearly 100,000-acre (40,469-hectare) tract of land they called Wachovia. There, the men began to build the village of Bethabara. Eventually, the Moravians would develop six villages on this land. The town of Salem, founded in 1766, became the administrative, spiritual, and craft center of the settlement.

Today, Salem is still a thriving village. Located near downtown Winston-Salem, the village is known as Old Salem. A living history museum, Old Salem is a popular tourist destination. Men and women dress in period costume to create the same types of crafts and goods that the Moravians produced in the 1700s. Visitors are encouraged to participate in hands-on activities, including making *scherenschnitte* (complicated cutout paper designs), cooking in fireplaces, and writing with quill pens. One of the more popular attractions in Old Salem is Winkler's Bakery. Built in 1800 and operated by Christian Winkler, the bakery produces goods from many of the same recipes it used in the nineteenth century.

In 1941, the United States entered World War II. Nearly nine thousand North Carolinians lost their lives in the war. Twenty-four major military installations around the state, including Fort Bragg, Cherry Point, and Camp Lejeune, trained soldiers for battle, built and maintained military equipment, and treated wounded soldiers returning home.

In 1960, black college students sat at an all-white lunch counter in Greensboro, launching a series of sit-ins that fueled the civil rights movement.

The Civil Rights Movement

Even though the Civil War ended slavery in 1865, racial discrimination against African Americans was still very much evident in the mid-1950s. African Americans in the South were denied the right to vote, and they faced discrimination when it came to finding housing and being hired for jobs. Public transportation, public schools, and even public restrooms were segregated.

On February 1, 1960, four young African American men from the North Carolina Agricultural and Technical College sat down at an all-white lunch counter in a Greensboro Woolworth's store and ordered lunch. The store's manager refused to serve them, and the students refused to give up their seats. They stayed until the store closed. The next day, the young men returned with twenty-five other students. By the third day of the protest, three hundred African Americans had arrived at the Woolworth's lunch counter. These kinds of peaceful protests became known as sit-ins. After the Greensboro sit-in, these types of protests spread to lunch counters across the United States and had a large influence on the outcome of the civil rights movement.

Into the Future

North Carolina is a state that is constantly looking forward. In 1959, business, university, and government leaders near Raleigh established Research Triangle Park (RTP). RTP was designed to attract organizations actively engaged in research that would benefit North Carolina's economy. To make the area even more enticing to potential businesses, large research institutions such as Duke University, North Carolina Central, North Carolina State University, and the University of North Carolina at Chapel Hill are also located in the area. Today, RTP is home to more than 170 research companies, including IBM, Sony Ericsson, and the U.S. Environmental Protection Agency (EPA).

Another program, called Smart Start, began in North Carolina in 1993. Smart Start is designed to provide all children in the state under the age of six with early education and health care. These services make sure that all North Carolina children are prepared to start kindergarten on time. The Smart Start program is now used as a model for other states' early education programs.

Chapter 3

THE GOVERNMENT OF NORTH CAROLINA

At the state level, North Carolina is governed much like the United States is at the federal level. There are three branches of the state government: the executive branch, the legislative branch, and the judicial branch. North Carolina is comprised of one hundred separate counties, each of which has its own governmental bodies.

The Executive Branch

The state's executive branch consists of the Office of the Governor, the Office of the Lieutenant Governor, and nineteen other departments. The governor is the leader of the executive branch. Governors serve four-year terms. If something happens to the governor during his or her term of service, the lieutenant governor takes over. The lieutenant governor and eight department heads, including the state treasurer, the secretary of state, and the heads of the departments of agriculture, labor, and public instruction, are also elected officials that serve four-year terms. The governor appoints the other eleven department heads.

Along with making sure that its departments are running smoothly, the executive branch proposes policies to the legislative branch. These policies affect state services such as health care, law

North Carolina's legislative branch is made up of a 50-member senate and 120-member house of representatives. Known as the general assembly, this government branch holds its meetings in the State Legislative Building.

enforcement, and education. It signs policies that are passed through the legislative branch into law, and it makes sure that the judicial branch enforces the laws of the state.

The Legislative Branch

The legislative branch of the state government is the general assembly. There are two parts to the general assembly: the senate and the house of representatives. There are 50 members of North Carolina's state senate and 120 members of the state's house of representatives. Representatives are elected every two years.

The state legislature usually meets once a year. However, if there is an issue that needs to be addressed right away, the governor can call an extra meeting called a special session. The legislative branch is responsible for introducing and passing bills into law. Once a bill has been proposed and discussed, members of the house or the senate vote on it. If the bill passes in one chamber, it is then sent to the other chamber to be discussed and voted on. After a bill is passed by both the senate and the house, it goes on to the governor's office.

If the governor agrees that the bill is in the best interest of the people of the state, he or she will sign it into law. If the governor disagrees, he or she can veto the bill. When the governor vetoes a bill, it is sent back to the chamber that introduced it. If three-fifths of the members of the house or senate vote to override the veto, the bill is passed to the other chamber. Three-fifths of the members of the other chamber must also vote to disregard the veto for the bill to be passed into law.

The Judicial Branch

It is the responsibility of the judicial branch to enforce the laws passed by the general assembly and the governor. Each county seat, and a few of the larger cities and towns, has two courts: a district court and a superior court. The district courts hear civil cases such as divorce and child custody cases, as well as minor disputes. Criminal cases involving misdemeanor offenses and juveniles are also heard by the district court. In district court cases, the judge makes the decisions. District court judges are elected every four years. More serious felony criminal cases are tried in superior court. These cases are presided over by a superior court judge and heard by a twelve-member jury. Superior court judges serve eight-year terms.

If the accused does not agree with the ruling at the district court or superior court level, the case may be appealed in the court of

PAST AND PRESENT

North Carolina's State Capitals

From 1765 to 1771, a man named William Tryon (1729–1788) was appointed by the English crown to govern North Carolina. Tryon established the waterfront town of New Bern as the colonial capital. Between 1767 and 1770, the first permanent capitol building, Tryon Palace, was built in what is now downtown New Bern. The building was also intended to serve as the Tryon family's home. However, only a year after the mansion's completion, Governor Tryon was reassigned to be the governor of New York, and he and his family moved away. In his place, the English king appointed Josiah Martin as governor. In 1775, at the beginning of the American Revolution, patriots attacked Tryon Palace and forced Martin to flee. The American patriots took over the building and began planning their new independent state. In February 1798, a fire started in the basement of the building and Tryon Palace was destroyed.

The capital of North Carolina was moved from New Bern to Raleigh in 1794. A new capitol building was built in Raleigh's central square, but that building burned down in 1831. Two years later, construction began on the current capitol building, which was completed in 1840. For forty-eight years, this building housed all of North Carolina's governmental bodies. In 1888, the supreme court and the state library moved to a different building.

Today, the general assembly is housed in its own building, known as the State Legislative Building. The legislature moved to this building in 1963. The state capitol houses the governor and his or her immediate staff.

Present-day New Bern is a bustling coastal town, and Tryon Palace has been restored to its former elegance. The mansion contains period furniture and art, and it's surrounded by gardens. Tryon Palace and its gardens are open to the public for guided tours.

appeals. Consisting of fifteen judges, this court reviews decisions made by the lower court and decides if these decisions should be upheld or overturned. Judges that sit on the court of appeals are elected to eight-year terms. If the accused still does not believe the courts' rulings are fair, he or she can appeal to one last court at the state level—the state's supreme court. The supreme court is the state's highest court. The decision of the seven justices on this court is final. Supreme court justices are also elected to eight-year terms.

Built in 1892 and renovated in the 1980s, the New Hanover County Courthouse, located in downtown Wilmington, still houses the county's district and superior courts.

Local Government

North Carolina is divided up into one hundred counties. Each county's citizens elect a county board of commissioners. Depending on the county, the board of commissioners may consist of anywhere between two and seven members. Members of the board of commissioners serve a two- to four-year term. The town or city where the county's government meets and conducts business is called the county seat.

Completed in 1840, the North Carolina State Capitol once housed all three of the state's governmental branches. Today, only the offices of the executive branch are housed in the building.

Much like the state's counties, most cities and towns in North Carolina elect a group of people to oversee the municipality's business. Depending on the city, this group may be called the board of commissioners, the board of aldermen, or simply the council. In most places, a mayor is also elected by the people of the municipality. The mayor is usually the head of the city council and is its spokesperson.

Chapter 4

THE ECONOMY OF NORTH CAROLINA

North Carolina has a wide variety of industries that create jobs for the state's population. Some of these industries, such as farming and textile manufacturing, have sustained the state for a long time. In addition, high-technology industries, such as aviation, telecommunications, and biotechnology, have moved into the state.

Agriculture

About half the income that North Carolina derives from agriculture comes from livestock. Farmers raise hogs, broilers, and turkeys. Hogs are the state's leading livestock product, and North Carolina is second in hog production in the country behind Iowa. North Carolina is also second in the production of turkeys (after Minnesota) and is the fourth largest producer of broilers (chickens that are between five and twelve weeks of age).

The other half of the state's farm income comes from crops such as corn, cotton, soybeans, and tobacco. North Carolina farms are the nation's leading producers of tobacco and sweet potatoes. The state is also the second largest producer of Christmas trees behind Oregon. Apples are North Carolina's largest fruit crop. The state also produces blueberries, peaches, and strawberries.

North Carolina farmers raise more hogs than any other type of livestock, making the state second only to Iowa in hog production. In 2008, hog farmers generated more than $200 million.

Manufacturing

North Carolina has a thriving chemical manufacturing industry. Its pharmaceutical companies manufacture drugs, and its textile industry produces synthetic fibers, such as nylon and polyester. In fact, North Carolina textile companies manufacture a variety of crucial textile products, including the fabric for bulletproof vests and fire-resistant uniforms for firefighters. Tobacco products are North Carolina's leading manufactured goods.

Furniture is another important commodity that is produced in the state. Much of this industry is based around the city of High

Point. The High Point Furniture Manufacturing Company began producing furniture in 1889. In 1901, thirty-five furniture manufacturers banded together to organize the Southern Furniture Market. Today, the twice-yearly High Point Market is the largest furniture trade show in the world.

High Tech

North Carolina is home to nine research universities, including three large engineering schools. The University of North Carolina system consists of sixteen campuses scattered around the state. There are also thirty-six private institutions of higher learning.

Founded in 1887, North Carolina State University is one of the nine research universities that call North Carolina home. It is the state's largest four-year institution.

North Carolina has the third largest community college system in the United States, with fifty-eight schools.

More than 520 biotechnology companies are located in North Carolina. A few of the bioscience and pharmaceutical companies in the state include Bayer, Merck, GlaxoSmithKline, and Novo Nordisk. With more than three thousand telecommunication, networking, and software development companies based in North Carolina, the state is also a major force in the information technology field. The largest U.S. facility for the computer giant IBM is located in Research Triangle Park. Charlotte houses the second largest

Aviation in North Carolina

In 1903, Orville Wright (1871–1948) and his brother, Wilbur (1867–1912), designed and flew the first heavier-than-air, mechanically powered airplane near the town of Kitty Hawk, North Carolina. The brothers, bicycle shop owners from Dayton, Ohio, began experimenting with flying machine designs only four years before. They quickly realized that if they were to be successful in manned flight, they needed an area with steady winds, flat expanses of land, and sandy soil that would afford them relatively soft landings.

After considering numerous locations, the brothers determined that a huge sand dune, called Kill Devil Hill, located just outside of Kitty Hawk, was the perfect location to conduct further experiments. On December 17, 1903, Orville successfully flew the airplane 120 feet (37 m) along the sand. That first flight lasted for a mere twelve seconds. Over the course of the day, the brothers took turns making three more flights. By the time they finished, Wilbur had logged the longest flight. The plane traveled 852 feet (260 m) over land, and the flight lasted nearly one minute.

Today, this feat is commemorated with the Wright Brothers National Memorial in Kill Devil Hills. It is also celebrated on the state's commemorative quarter, which was released by the U.S. Mint in 2001. The license plates on North Carolina's automobiles mark the event with the words "First in Flight." After the brothers' historic feat, they went on to outstanding careers in aviation. North Carolina continues its legacy of aviation excellence by hosting four international, seventy-four domestic, and three hundred private airports. In addition, it is home to more than 160 aerospace and aviation companies. Seven of the top ten largest global air defense companies, including Boeing, Lockheed Martin, and Raytheon, call the state home.

Microsoft campus behind the one in Washington. Other large technology companies with a presence in North Carolina include Cisco Systems, Dell, Google, and SAS.

Other Industries

Aquaculture, or raising fish in artificial ponds, is an important industry in the state. Fish farms in North Carolina produce Atlantic menhaden, catfish, crayfish, and trout. In addition, North Carolina fishermen catch blue crabs, clams, flounder, and shrimp.

Charlotte, the second largest financial center in the United States behind New York City, has become known as Wall Street South.

Banking, insurance, and real estate are some of the state's most important service industries. Several large banking companies, including Bank of America and Wachovia, are headquartered in Charlotte, making the city the second largest financial center in the United States behind New York.

North Carolina is also home to many professional and college sports teams. However, sports are not the only entertainment that the state provides. A number of movies and television shows have been filmed or produced in the state. In fact, North Carolina is often called Hollywood East. North Carolina also offers numerous concerts, theater productions, and outdoor attractions to entertain tourists and residents alike.

Chapter 5

PEOPLE FROM NORTH CAROLINA: PAST AND PRESENT

Over the years, many famous people have called North Carolina home. Some were born in the state, while others moved there as children or adults. Three presidents, Andrew Jackson, Andrew Johnson, and James Polk, were born in North Carolina. The state has also produced its share of artists, musicians, authors, and inventors. No matter whether these people are North Carolinians by birth or by choice, they have all had a major effect on the culture of the state and of the country.

Clay Aiken (1978–) Clay Aiken, runner-up on the second season of the hit television show *American Idol* in 2003, was born Clayton Holmes Grissom in Raleigh. He adopted Aiken, his mother's maiden name, as his stage name. Since his appearance on *American Idol*, Aiken has released five albums. In October 2003, his debut album, *Measure of a Man*, quickly became a bestseller. It earned Aiken the Fan's Choice Award at the 31st Annual American Music Awards.

Maya Angelou (1928–) Maya Angelou is a celebrated poet, novelist, and educator. She was born in St. Louis, Missouri.

The celebrated poet and novelist Maya Angelou lives in Winston-Salem, North Carolina, where she has taught American studies at Wake Forest University for nearly thirty years.

Her autobiography *I Know Why the Caged Bird Sings* was published in 1970 and nominated for a National Book Award. In 1972, she wrote the screenplay and musical score for the film *Georgia, Georgia,* which was nominated for a Pulitzer Prize. Today, Angelou is a resident of Winston-Salem, where she teaches American studies at Wake Forest University.

Caleb Bradham (1867–1934) Caleb Bradham was a pharmacist in New Bern in the late 1800s. Concerned with people's health, Bradham set out to produce a healthy soda.

The Eastern Band of Cherokee Indians

When Europeans first arrived in North Carolina, many Native American tribes lived in the area. One of these tribes was the Cherokee Indians. In the 1830s, the U.S. government forced the Cherokee, and other Native Americans, to give up their land east of the Mississippi River. The government made them relocate to what is now Oklahoma. During this migration, which has since become known as the Trail of Tears, many Cherokee died from starvation and exposure to the cold. However, not all of them left their land. Some, including a Cherokee chief named Yonaguska, or Drowning Bear, hid in the mountains of North Carolina instead. At that time, Native Americans were not allowed to own land. Chief Yonaguska's adopted son, Will Thomas, a white man, bought land and allowed his father to live on it. Upon Chief Yonaguska's death, Thomas was made chief of the Cherokee, the first and only white man to ever hold that position.

Today, the Eastern Band of Cherokee Indians is the only federally recognized tribe in North Carolina. They are descendants of those Cherokee who refused to leave their land. The tribe makes their home on a 110-square-mile (285-square-kilometer) area called the Qualla Boundary, which is located in the western part of the state. Currently, there are approximately thirteen thousand members of the Eastern Band of Cherokee Indians, about nine thousand of which live in the Qualla Boundary. The tribe has its own elected government officials. The executive branch is made up of the principal chief and the vice chief; both serve four-year terms. Members of the legislative tribal council and the judicial branch serve two-year terms. During the summer months, many people visit the Boundary to attend the popular outdoor drama *Unto These Hills*. This play depicts the history of the Cherokee people in North Carolina.

By mixing different juices, syrups, and spices, he developed a concoction known as Brad's Drink. Later, Bradham changed the name to Pepsi-Cola. The sweet drink quickly spread throughout the nation.

John Coltrane (1926–1967)
John Coltrane was born on September 23, 1926, in Hamlet, North Carolina, a town about 80 miles (129 km) east of Charlotte. Surrounded by music from a young age, Coltrane soon developed an interest in playing the clarinet. Later, influenced by such jazz musicians as Johnny Hodges, Charlie Parker, and Lester Young, he switched to

John Coltrane, a talented jazz saxophonist, died of liver disease in 1967 at the age of forty-one.

the saxophone. A legendary musician, Coltrane recorded a number of albums and played with other jazz greats, including Dizzy Gillespie, Miles Davis, and Thelonious Monk.

Sarah Dessen (1970–) Sarah Dessen is the author of such popular young adult books as *Just Listen* and *The Truth About Forever*. She was raised in Chapel Hill, where both of her parents taught at the University of North Carolina at

Chapel Hill. Dessen graduated with a degree in English from the university in 1993 and currently teaches creative writing there.

James Buchanan Duke (1856–1925) James Buchanan Duke, born near Durham, was the second son of tobacco industrialist Washington Duke. The Duke family began to farm, manufacture, and market tobacco products shortly after the Civil War. In 1890, the five largest tobacco companies merged, becoming the American Tobacco Company, with James Duke as president. The Duke family established a trust fund to donate money to those who were less fortunate. In 1924, North Carolina's Trinity College was renamed Duke University in honor of the family.

Roberta Flack (1937–) Born in Asheville, Roberta Flack is a Grammy Award–winning singer and songwriter. One of her most loved songs, "The First Time Ever I Saw Your Face," won the 1973 Grammy for Song of the Year. Flack won a second Grammy the following year for the song "Killing Me Softly with His Song."

O. Henry (1862–1910) William Sydney Porter, the famed short-story author, is probably better known by his pseudonym, O. Henry. Born in Greensboro, Porter moved to Texas at the age of twenty and worked as a ranch hand and bank teller. In 1896, he was accused, tried, and convicted of stealing money from the bank. While serving time in prison, Porter wrote about a dozen short stories under the name O.

An avid reader, O. Henry began writing short stories while incarcerated. By the time he died at the age of forty-seven, he had penned more than three hundred short stories.

Henry. Wishing to distance himself from his past, he permanently changed his name to O. Henry when he was released. The author then moved to New York City, where he would eventually publish more than three hundred short stories, including "The Gift of the Magi," before his death.

Thomas Wolfe (1900–1938) Thomas Wolfe was a novelist as well as a short-story author who was born in North Carolina. His novel *Look Homeward, Angel* portrays his childhood in his hometown of Asheville. There, his mother, Julia, ran a boarding house called the Old Kentucky Home. The house is now being operated as a historic literary landmark, with guided tours and writing workshops available.

Timeline

1587	The first English settlers arrive at Roanoke Island on the Outer Banks.
1590	John White returns to Roanoke to find the colonists gone.
1653	The first permanent English settlers arrive from Virginia.
1710	The Carolina colony is split into northern and southern sections.
1789	North Carolina becomes the twelfth state in the Union.
1828	Andrew Jackson is elected as the seventh president of the United States.
1845	James Polk becomes the eleventh president of the United States.
1861	North Carolina officially secedes from the Union.
1865	Andrew Johnson becomes the seventeenth president of the United States.
1868	North Carolina is readmitted to the Union.
1903	The Wright brothers make the first successful heavier-than-air flight at Kitty Hawk.
1918	Fort Bragg is established.
1954	Hurricane Hazel slams into North Carolina's coast.
1959	Research Triangle Park opens.
1960	Sit-ins take place at the Woolworth's lunch counter in Greensboro.
1989	Hurricane Hugo slams North Carolina's coast, causing damage as far inland as Charlotte.
1993	The Smart Start program begins.
1995	The Carolina Panthers football team takes the field for the first time.
1997	The Hartford Whalers hockey team moves from Connecticut to North Carolina and changes its name to the Hurricanes.
2006	The Carolina Hurricanes win the Stanley Cup.
2008	The movies *Nights in Rodanthe* and *The Secret Life of Bees* are filmed in North Carolina.
2009	The North Carolina Tar Heels win the NCAA championship.

State motto:	"To Be, Rather Than to Seem"
State capital:	Raleigh
State flower:	Dogwood
State bird:	Cardinal
State tree:	Pine
State insect:	European honey bee
State fruit:	Scuppernong grape
State vegetable:	Sweet potato
Statehood date and number:	November 21, 1789; twelfth state
State nicknames:	The Tar Heel State and the Old North State
Total area and U.S. rank:	53,821 square miles (13,939,575 square km); twenty-eighth largest state
Population:	8,049,000
Length of coastline:	301 miles (484 km)

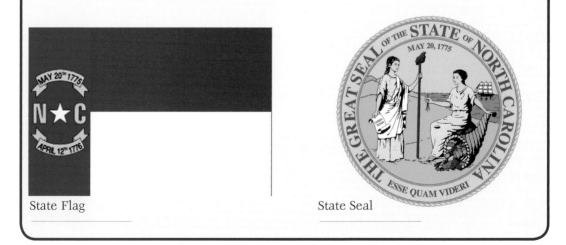

State Flag

State Seal

Highest elevation:	Mount Mitchell, at 6,684 feet (2,037 m)
Lowest elevation:	Sea level, at the Atlantic Ocean
Major rivers:	Cape Fear River, Neuse River, Roanoke River, Yadkin River
Major lakes:	Lake Mattamuskeet, Lake Norman, Lake Phelps, Lake Waccamaw
Highest recorded temperature:	110°F (43°C) in Fayetteville, August 21, 1983
Lowest recorded temperature:	-34°F (-37°C) at Mount Mitchell, January 25, 1985
Origin of state name:	From the Latin word *Carolus*, in honor of King Charles I of England
Chief agricultural products:	Corn, cotton, soybeans, tobacco, livestock
Major industries:	Manufacturing, research and development, banking, film

Cardinal

Dogwood

abolish To end or do away with a practice or system.

aquaculture The practice of raising fish in artificial ponds; also called fish farming.

aviation The science of flying man-made aircraft.

bill A draft of a law presented to the legislature for a vote.

commodity An object or product that can be sold or traded for profit.

endangered In danger of dying out.

felony A serious or severe crime.

manufacturing The process of making useful products from raw materials.

musket An early form of firearm. Muskets were eventually replaced by more accurate firearms such as rifles.

patriot A person who is very proud of, and very loyal to, his or her country.

persecution The mistreatment of a person or a group of people based on their race, religion, or beliefs.

segregated Divided by race, like the public facilities in the American South until the mid-twentieth century.

settler A person who travels to a new region or territory in order to establish a home.

sit-in A form of peaceful protest in which participants occupy seats at a place that practices racial discrimination or another social injustice.

sound A large, shallow body of water.

tar A black, sticky liquid used during colonial times to coat wooden ships to keep them from rotting.

wetlands Areas of land that are usually saturated with water.

veto To block a decision.

Eastern Band of Cherokee Indians

498 Tsali Boulevard

Cherokee, NC 28719

(800) 438-1601

Web site: http://www.cherokee-nc.com

The Eastern Band of Cherokee Indians provides information about events in the Qualla Boundary, including the outdoor drama *Unto These Hills*.

North Carolina Civil War Tourism Council

P.O. Box 844

Goldsboro, NC 27533

Web site: http://www.nccivilwar.com

The North Carolina Civil War Tourism Council educates the public about what life was like during the Civil War, and it helps preserve the state's Civil War–era sites.

North Carolina Maritime Museum

315 Front Street

Beaufort, NC 28516-2125

(252) 728-7317

Web site: http://www.ncmaritime.org

The North Carolina Maritime Museum researches, preserves, and documents the history, culture, and environment of coastal North Carolina.

North Carolina Museum of History

5 East Edenton Street

Raleigh, NC 27601-1011

(919) 807-7900

Web site: http://ncmuseumofhistory.org

The North Carolina Museum of History collects and preserves historical materials that relate to North Carolina's history and makes them available to the public through exhibits, publications, and educational programs.

North Carolina Office of Archives & History

109 E. Jones Street

Raleigh, NC 27601

(919) 807-7280

Web site: http://www.history.ncdcr.gov

The North Carolina Office of Archives & History collects and preserves the state's historic documents.

Old Salem Museums and Gardens

600 South Main Street

Winston-Salem, NC 27101

(336) 721-7300

Web site: http://www.oldsalem.org

The Old Salem Museums and Gardens is a living history museum that includes authentic buildings, craftspeople, and a collection of antiques that depict life in early North Carolina.

Web Sites

Due to the changing nature of Internet links, Rosen Publishing has developed an online list of Web sites related to the subject of this book. This site is updated regularly. Please use this link to access the list:

http://www.rosenlinks.com/uspp/ncpp

FOR FURTHER READING

Angelou, Maya, and Edwin Graves Wilson, ed. *Poetry for Young People: Maya Angelou.* New York, NY: Sterling, 2007.

Boyd, Bentley. *Tar Heel Tales*. Williamsburg, VA: Chester Comix, 2005.

Cannavale, Matthew. *Voices from Colonial America: North Carolina 1524–1776.* Washington, DC: National Geographic Children's Books, 2007.

Conley, Robert J. *A Cherokee Encyclopedia*. Albuquerque, NM: University of New Mexico Press, 2007.

Conley, Robert J. *The Cherokee Nation*. Albuquerque, NM: University of New Mexico Press, 2005.

Dunn, Joe. *The Wright Brothers.* Edina, MN: ABDO Publishing Company, 2008.

Grant, Gerald. *Hope and Despair in the American City: Why There Are No Bad Schools in Raleigh.* Cambridge, MA: Harvard University Press, 2009.

Heinrichs, Ann. *North Carolina.* New York, NY: Children's Press, 2008.

McDowell, Marilyn Taylor. *Carolina Harmony.* New York, NY: Delacorte Press, 2009.

Miller, Jake. *The Lost Colony of Roanoke: A Primary Source History.* New York, NY: Rosen Publishing Group, 2006.

Mis, Melody. *The Colony of North Carolina: A Primary Source History.* New York, NY: Rosen Publishing Group, 2006.

Ratliff, Ben. *Coltrane: The Story of a Sound.* New York, NY. Farrar, Straus and Giroux, 2007.

Reed, Jennifer. *Cape Hatteras National Seashore: Adventure, Explore, Discover.* Berkeley Heights, NJ: Enslow Publishers, Inc., 2008.

Smith, Rich. *North Carolina.* Edina, MN: ABDO Publishing Company, 2009.

Zepke, Terrance. *Pirates of the Carolinas.* Sarasota, FL: Pineapple Press, 2009.

BIBLIOGRAPHY

Eastern Band of Cherokee Indians in North Carolina. "Cherokee History and Culture." Retrieved September 30, 2009 (http://www.cherokee-nc.com/index.php?page=56).

Nature Conservancy. "The Nature Conservancy in North Carolina." Retrieved September 30, 2009 (http://www.nature.org/wherewework/northamerica/states/northcarolina).

North Carolina Biotechnology Center. "Biotechnology in NC." Retrieved September 30, 2009 (http://www.ncbiotech.org/biotechnology_in_nc).

North Carolina Business History. "Overview of NC Business Development." Retrieved September 30, 2009 (http://www.historync.org).

North Carolina Department of Commerce. "Quick NC Facts." Retrieved September 30, 2009 (http://www.nccommerce.com/en/AboutNorthCarolina/NCQuickFacts).

North Carolina General Assembly. "How a Law Is Made." Retrieved September 30, 2009 (http://www.ncleg.net/NCGAInfo/Bill-Law/bill-law.html).

North Carolina History Project. "North Carolina Encyclopedia." Retrieved September 30, 2009 (http://www.northcarolinahistory.org).

Old Salem Museums and Gardens. "Town of Salem." Retrieved September 30, 2009 (http://www.oldsalem.org/index.php?id=48).

Smithsonian National Air and Space Museum. "1903 Wright Flyer." Retrieved September 30, 2009 (http://www.nasm.si.edu/exhibitions/gal100/wright1903.html).

State Climate Office of North Carolina. "North Carolina Climate." Retrieved September 30, 2009 (http://www.nc-climate.ncsu.edu/climate/ncclimate.html#temp).

State Library of North Carolina. "Military History." Retrieved September 30, 2009 (http://statelibrary.ncdcr.gov/colls/themes/july.html).

State Library of North Carolina. "The North Carolina Encyclopedia." Retrieved September 30, 2009 (http://statelibrary.ncdcr.gov/NC/COVER.htm).

Tryon Palace Historic Sites & Gardens. "Tryon Palace History." Retrieved September 30, 2009 (http://www.tryonpalace.org/history.html).

University of North Carolina at Chapel Hill Libraries. "Slavery in North Carolina." Retrieved September 30, 2009 (http://www.lib.unc.edu/stories/slavery).

University of North Carolina at Chapel Hill Libraries. "The Wilmington Ten." Retrieved September 30, 2009 (http://www.lib.unc.edu/ncc/ref/nchistory/feb2005/index.html).

U.S. National Park Service. "Great Smoky Mountains National Park." Retrieved September 30, 2009 (http://www.nps.gov/grsm/index.htm).

Whitaker, Gordon. "North Carolina Municipalities." *Local Government in North Carolina*. 2nd ed. 2003. Retrieved September 30, 2009 (http://www.sog.unc.edu/programs/civiced/ncccma/textrevised/chapter2.html).

INDEX

A

Aiken, Clay, 32
Angelou, Maya, 32–33
aviation, 27, 30

B

Bradham, Caleb, 33, 35

C

civil rights movement, 19–20
Civil War, 6, 16–17, 19, 36
Civilian Conservation Corps, 17
Coltrane, John, 35

D

Dessen, Sarah, 35–36
Duke, James Buchanan, 36
Duke University, 20, 36

E

Eastern Band of Cherokee Indians, 34

F

Flack, Roberta, 36
Fort Bragg, 19
Fugitive Slave Act, 16–17

G

Great Depression, 17

J

Jackson, Andrew, 32
Johnson, Andrew, 32

M

Mount Mitchell, 7–8, 11

N

North Carolina
  economy of, 27–31
  geography of, 5, 7–13
  government of, 21–26
  history of, 5–6, 10, 14–20, 24
  people from, 32–38

O

O. Henry, 36, 38
Old Salem, 18

P

Polk, James, 32

R

Research Triangle Park, 20, 29
Revolutionary War, 15, 24
Roanoke Island, 10
Roosevelt, Franklin D., 17

S

slavery, 16–17, 19
Smart Start program, 20

T

tobacco, 27, 28, 36
Trail of Tears, 34

U

University of North Carolina, 20, 29, 35

W

Wolfe, Thomas, 38
World War I, 17
World War II, 19
Wright brothers, 30

About the Author

Kristi Lew is the author of more than thirty science and social science books for teachers and young people. After graduating from North Carolina State University, Lew taught science at Athens Drive High School in Raleigh. She now lives in St. Petersburg, Florida, but visits family and friends in her home state often.

Photo Credits

Cover (top, left), pp. 16, 19 Library of Congress Prints and Photographs Division; cover (top, right) http://en.wikipedia.org/wiki/File:Downtown-Raleigh-from-Western-Boulevard-Overpass-20081012.jpeg; cover (bottom) http://en.wikipedia.org/wiki/File:Pilot_Mountain_US-52_in_NC_071102.JPG; pp. 3, 7, 14, 21, 27, 32, 39 http://en.wikipedia.org/wiki/File:Fayetteville_Street-27527.jpg; p. 4 © GeoAtlas; p. 8 http://en.wikipedia.org/wiki/Looking_Glass_Rock; p. 9 © www.istockphoto.com/William Britten; p. 11 © www.istockphoto.com/Denis Tangney Jr.; p. 13 © www.istockphoto.com/Jane Brennecker; p. 15 © The Trustees of The British Museum/Art Resource, NY; pp. 22, 28, 31 © AP Images; p. 25 © www.istockphoto.com/Katherine Welles; pp. 26, 29 © www.istockphoto.com/Matej Krajocovic; p. 33 Jemal Countess/Getty Images; p. 35 Michael Ochs Archives/Getty Images; p. 37 Hulton Archive/Getty Images; p. 40 (left) Courtesy of Robesus, Inc.; p. 41 (left) http://upload.wikimedia.org/wikipedia/en/d/da/Cardinal.jpg; p. 41 (right) © www.istockphoto.com/Oscar Gutierrez.

Designer: Les Kanturek; Photo Researcher: Amy Feinberg